I'm a Pill Bug

DUE

Written by
Yukihisa Tokuda

Illustrated by
Kiyoshi Takahashi

Kane/Miller
BOOK PUBLISHERS

Hello!
Do you know what this is?
Do you know who I am?
A ball?

No, not a ball.

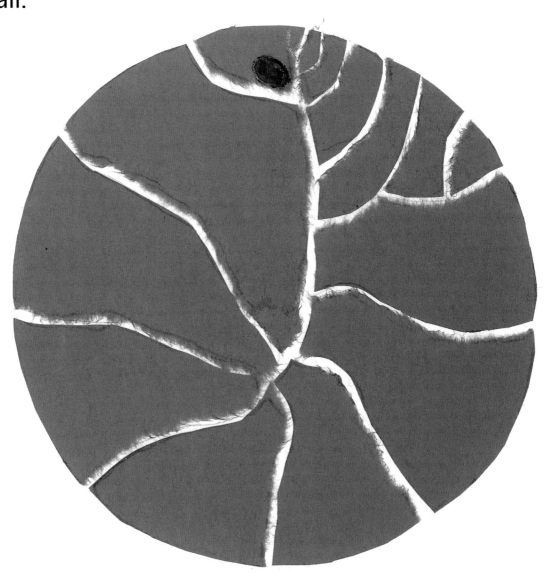

I'm a pill bug!
(This is how big I really am.)

I live in the garden with my family.
Our home is underneath this flower pot.

Pill bugs like to live close to people.
Do you know why? Shall I tell you?

At night, we leave our homes to eat.
We eat lots of different things – dead plants,
dead bugs, and leftover human food.
We also like pet food, newspapers and cardboard.
Because we eat all kinds of things, some people
call us "the scavengers of nature."

Our appetite is huge.
We can eat leaves as big as this.
As soon as we eat, we poop (lots and
lots of square-shaped poop).

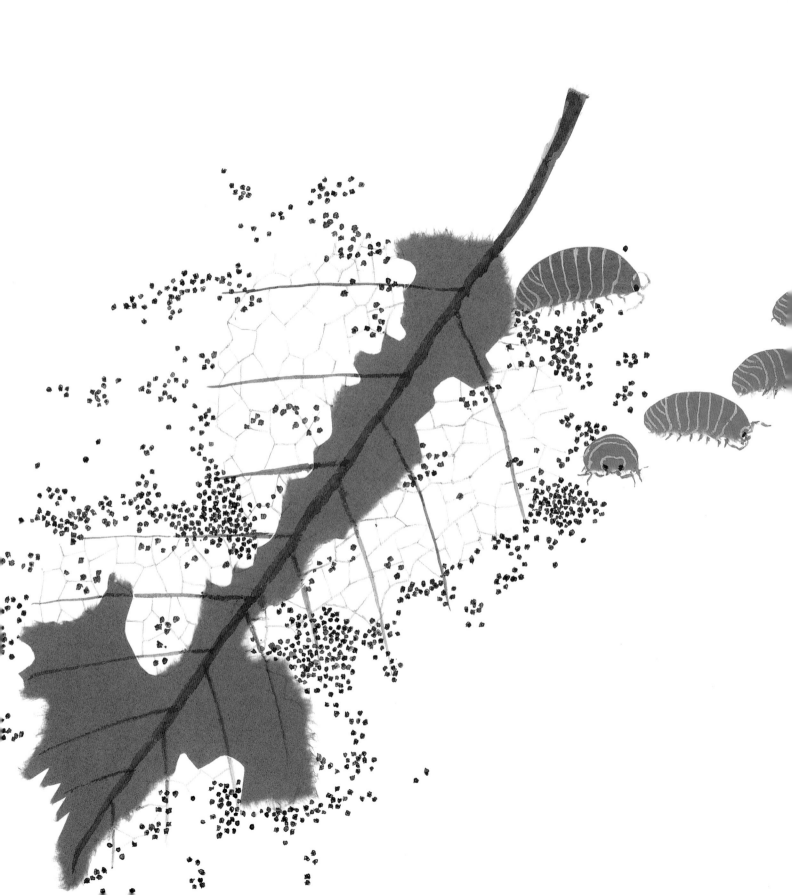

We also eat some things you might think are strange.
Can you guess what they are?
Stones and concrete!
We need to eat them now and then, or our bodies
don't work properly.
That's why we need to live near people, and their
concrete sidewalks, walls and buildings!

We have many neighbors who frighten us.
Today, while I was walking in the flower bed, I saw an ant.

Ants are small but scary.
Don't worry! We have a special way to defend ourselves.

On the count of three: one, two, three!
Ta-da! I roll myself into a ball!
My hard shell protects my body and keeps me safe.
See? The ant gives up and goes away.

Unfortunately, it doesn't help with frogs, lizards, or birds.
They can still eat us, even when we're rolled up.
We just try to stay away from them.

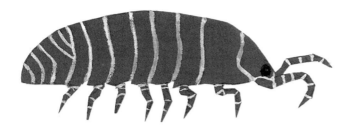 

Some neighbors are friendly though.
These wood lice look very much like us,
but they can't roll up.
Poor things!

We shed our shells many times as we gradually grow bigger.
It's like taking off a shirt that's all of a sudden too small.
The way we shed our shells is very interesting.
First, we shed the rear half.

Then, the next day, we shed the front half.
And we never forget to eat the old shell!
Yum! Very nutritious.

When we're grown-up, we find mates and lay eggs.
Mother pill bugs lay eggs in thick films which they
carry, very carefully, under their tummies.

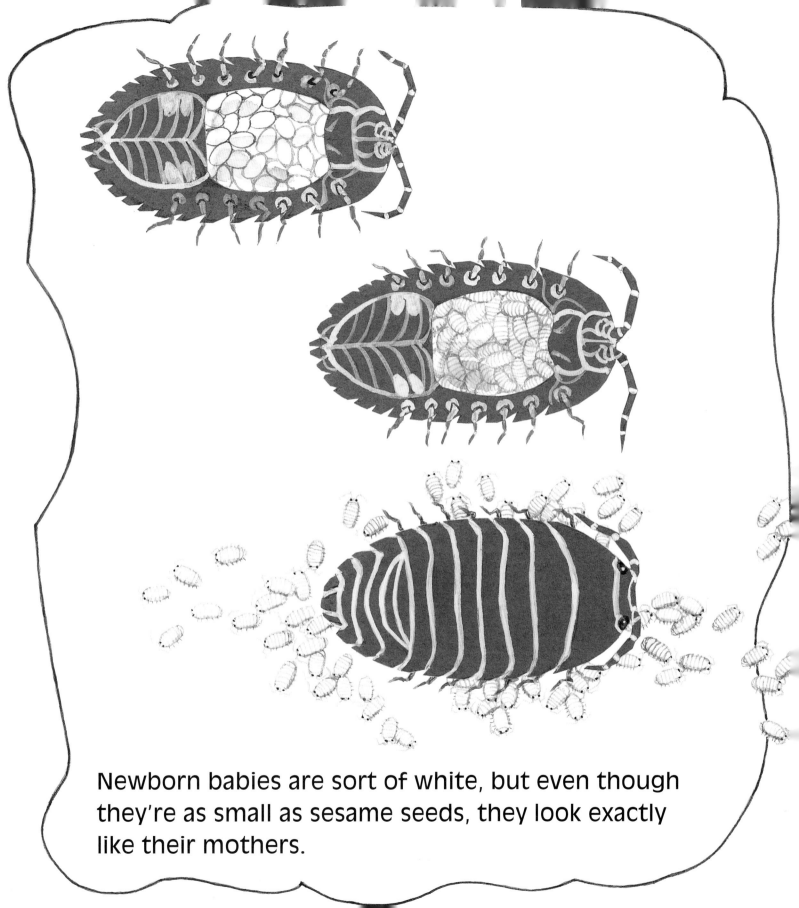

Newborn babies are sort of white, but even though they're as small as sesame seeds, they look exactly like their mothers.

By the way, you don't think we're insects, do you?
Of course you don't! Look at our legs. Insects have
six legs. We have a lot more than six!

No, we're not insects. We're related to crabs and shrimp.
I'm not sure, but maybe that's the reason we can swim a
little bit...if we accidentally fall in the water.

We don't like the cold.
So, towards the end of fall,
we all dig down into the ground
and sleep until spring arrives.

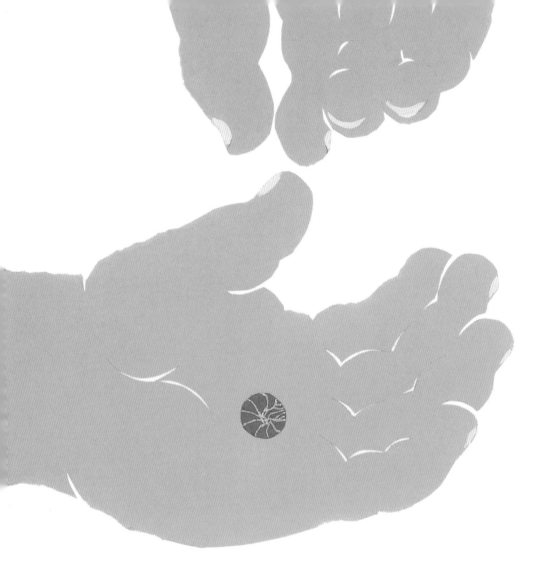

Now you know some things about pill bugs.
If you want to know more, just look for us.
You can find us in your garden at home (if you have one),
or in the park.
And I'm sure some of us live near your school.
If you see us you can touch us – but gently, please!

Want an even closer look?
Put some soil in a plastic container,
and add some leaves on top.
Don't forget a bit of concrete or stone!
Then, find a pill bug to come for a visit.
He'll need you to mist him with water once in a while.
(You wouldn't want him to dry up.)
It's easy to have a pill bug as your guest.

One more thing though. At the end of fall,
would you please bring your pill bug
back to the place where you found him?
He'll want to be with his family
during the cold winter!

Hope to see you soon!